FROM THE FIRE

ANGELA POLLOCK

From the Fire
Copyright © 2016 by Angela M. Pollock
All rights reserved. No part of this book may be reproduced or transmitted in any form or by any means without written permission of the author.

ISBN-13: 978-0-9968715-4-9

Printed in the United States of America

RevMedia Publishing
PO BOX 5172, Kingwood, TX 77325

No part of this book may be reproduced or transmitted in any form or by any means, electronic or mechanical–including photocopying, recording, or by any information storage and retrieval system–without permission in writing from the publisher.

Unless otherwise noted, all Scripture quotations are taken from THE HOLY BIBLE, NEW INTERNATIONAL VERSION®, NIV® Copyright © 1973, 1978, 1984, 2011 by Biblica, Inc.® Used by permission. All rights reserved worldwide.

Scripture quotations marked (KJV) are taken from the Holy Bible King James Version. In the public domain.

Scripture quotations marked (NASB) are taken from the NEW AMERICAN STANDARD BIBLE®, Copyright © 1960,1962,1963,1968,1971,1972,1973,1975,1977,1995 by The Lockman Foundation. Used by permission.

Scripture quotations marked (NKJV) are taken from the New King James Version®. Copyright © 1982 by Thomas Nelson. Used by permission. All rights reserved.

Photography by Al Torres Photography
(www.altorresphotography.com)
Houston, TX

Dedication

To my dear friend (since the fifth grade), Kami, who is going through the fire of cancer with astounding courage, grace, transparency, and even humor. She continues to lean hard on the chest of her Savior, all the while, serving her family and encouraging her friends. I believe she will emerge without the smell of smoke and with a fiery testimony.

To my cousins, Jill and Michael. The heat of your trial is great, but His presence with you is greater. I am stronger by having you in my life. Your faith is a beacon. You are amazing and you're on His radar always. For your miracle, we stand.

To my five children: Adrien, Rebekah, Sarah-Grace, Riley, and Jacob, who keep my heart beating like a bongo drum! You are my greatest gifts and joys forever. Thank you for loving me in all your unique ways. We have fun! I'm forever in your corner and I love you.

To my first grandbaby, Wyatt. I love you, little rascal! God has some big plans for you, I am certain.

To my sweet family who embraces my dreams and my silliness. Thank you for your deep love, encouragement, and sacrifice. Mom, Dad, Monica, Jim, Bella, Zachary, and Marc—you have my heart.

To my precious friends with whom I am thankful to breathe in this life! You have held my hand and led me through the fog of recent seasons. You remind me of who I am, and Whose I am.

— I love you —

God Leads His Dear Children Along
George A. Young
1903
(www.popularhymns.com)
Bold, italics added

In shady, green pastures, so rich and so sweet,
God leads His dear children along;
Where the water's cool flow bathes the weary one's feet,
God leads His dear children along.

Some through the waters, some through the flood,
Some through the fire, but all through the blood;
Some through great sorrow, but God gives a song,
In the night season and all the day long.

Sometimes on the mount where the sun shines so bright,
God leads His dear children along;
Sometimes in the valley, in darkest of night,
God leads His dear children along.

Though sorrows befall us and evils oppose,
God leads His dear children along;
Through grace we can conquer, defeat all our foes,
God leads His dear children along.

Away from the mire, and away from the clay,
God leads His dear children along;
Away up in glory, eternity's day,
God leads His dear children along.

Contents

Introduction

Chapter 1
See Him in the Fire

Chapter 2
Have your Senses Trained in the Fire

Chapter 3
Worship in the Fire

Chapter 4
Stay Low in the Fire

Chapter 5
Obey His Direction in the Fire

Chapter 6
Don't Waste the Fire

Closing Words and a Personal Invitation

About the Author

Endorsements

Acknowledgements

Thank you to Joan Hunter of Joan Hunter Ministries, my friend and mentor. She is a humble leader and one of the busiest women I know in ministry, but she always finds time to return my texts and pray (even if she is on the other side of the world, ministering to the hurting).

Thank you to David Yanez and Ted Bragg, with RevMedia Network for all of your help and great work in publishing this book.

Thank you to Jeanette Morris for your expertise and patience in editing. (http://www.firstimpressionswriting.com)

Thank you to my pastors, Jeff and Eileen Hackleman (Family Faith Church) for all that you do and for who you are. You are unwavering in the love of God and the fruits of His Spirit.

Thanks to pastors Rob and Jennifer Walker for your prayers and friendship.

Thank to my Conroe BFFs -Steph, Becca and Jen- for 'showing up' for me since 5th grade! Your kind hearts peak louder than any words I could.

And, foremost, thank you to the Fourth Man in My Fiery Furnace, my sweet Jesus!

I am forever thankful that He chased this Texas girl with His wild love and didn't stop until He caught me. He has never left me –

    through the fire,
    through the rain,

through the tears,
through the pain.

He is my confidante, strong tower, my Alpha and Omega!

Introduction

This is a message from my heart about coming out "From the Fire," with an emphasis on coming from it, out of the hard times, the trials, and the curveballs that cross our paths. It is a quick read, because I understand the busy days that we all are in. We are living in the days of acceleration in so many arenas. Things that took a decade to accomplish in the past will be completed in mere months. I believe we will hear truths and be set free quicker in order to set the pace, run the race, and bring others with us who could not reach their destinations on their own.

When people get hit with various hurts and circumstances in life, they often can get stuck in the place of their pain or confusion. I see it like a wounded bird in a cage. The door to the cage is opened, but the bird remains in the cage, just watching life pass it by, unable to fly out of that difficult place. Sometimes we can see a way of escape, but may not have the courage or strength to fly due to the tough season of life.

The good news is, we have an advocate, a helper, a healer, a friend, in the Lord. He sees all that you have been through and knows what you are feeling at this very moment. He has more than enough strength to share with His children. He is generous in all His ways. He will revive you in His love and bring you to new heights of freedom.

> "He giveth power to the faint; and to them that have no might he increaseth strength. Even the youths shall faint and be weary, and the young men shall utterly fall: But

> they that wait upon the Lord shall renew their strength; they shall mount up with wings as eagles; they shall run, and not be weary; and they shall walk, and not faint."
> (Isaiah 40:29-31, KJV)

You are called to be more than a conqueror in this place, in this race, in this life. Your life. You only get one. Why not make it count?

In this book I share some of my life journeys, where God wove His love into some tough places and taught me some powerful truths. I have found Him in the big and the little things in life. He is not too big to concern Himself with the little details of our lives. You hear a lot about how big God is, and yes, He is. But He is also in the little. He is in the little crevices in our lives, knows the number of hairs on our head, our individual thoughts, and our fingerprints. He collects our tears in a bottle.

I'm going to touch on six key points about being in the fire and coming out from the fire. I am believing for the Spirit of the Lord to touch you with His precious, fiery love, heal you with His power, and break chains off of you, even as you read.

Grab it, it's yours.

I decree that you will come out of your fire, without the smell of smoke, and run the course that He has set before you, with great zeal, strength, and joy.

You will fulfill the story He specifically wrote about your life.

> "Your eyes saw my unformed body; all the days ordained for me were written in your book before one of them came to be." (Psalm 139:16)

I know the best is yet to come for all of us!

> "But as it is written: Eye has not seen nor ear heard, nor have entered into the heart of man the things which God has prepared for those who love Him." (1 Corinthians 2:9 NKJV)

I pray that God would bless, heal, and strengthen everyone reading these pages. May He heal your heart of every hurt and trauma and call you out from the fire. May you come out, leaning upon His love. Amen.

Under Your Wings

Love to Thee, my dearest friend, my confidante in life.
You are closer than a brother
And nearer than a whisper.
Your love is life to me.

Enlarge my heart, to love you more,
To die to self and gain,
To bring the lost near your side,
And You'll heal away their pain.

Blessed Savior, deepest love...
I'll walk where you will lead.
For there is no darkness under your wings,
And there, my soul shall cling.

Angela Pollock
Inspired by Psalm 63

Chapter 1
See Him in the Fire

Sometimes, when the fire hits, when the storms come in our life, we think God is MIA (missing in action). He may be quiet at times, but He is near. He is close. God is a supernaturally natural God. He is not hidden behind a curtain like the Wizard of Oz. God wants to walk this life with you. He is as up-close and personal as you will let Him be. "Never will I leave you; never will I forsake you" (Hebrews 13:5b).

He is not far away and removed, watching from the heavens when you encounter trials.

> He is close.
> Closer than your heartbeat.
> He sees you,
> And
> He is with you in the fire.

In Daniel chapter 3, we read the story of Shadrach, Meshach, and Abednego. King Nebuchadnezzar commanded all people to bow down to the golden image. This image was ninety feet high and ninety feet wide. It wasn't a little gold statue like an Oscar award. Three courageous young men refused to worship any god except the one true God.

In Daniel 3:15, we read, "But if you do not worship the image, you will be thrown immediately into the blazing furnace. Then what god will be able to rescue you from my hand?' They replied, 'King Nebuchadnezzar, we do not need to defend ourselves before you in this matter. If we are thrown into the blazing furnace, the God we serve is able to deliver us from it, and He will deliver us from Your Majesty's hand. But even if He does not, we want you to know, Your Majesty, that we will not serve your gods or worship the image of gold you have set up."

I love the fact that Shadrach, Meshach and Abednego were willing to endure the fire, even if the God they trusted in did not deliver them. They had fire in their bellies. They were not politically correct with the king. They were literally prepared to give their bodies unto death, rather than worship a false god. Our allegiance to God must always trump allegiance to the world's system.

So often, people put conditions on their devotion and service to God. They pray: Lord, if you deliver me out of this mess, or Lord, when you answer this prayer of mine, I will get radical for you, etc. Those Hebrew boys were all in with God and the flames. No. Matter. What.

The three young, brave men were bound and thrown into the burning fiery furnace. When nothing happened to them, the king was enraged and heated the furnace seven times hotter. The servants whom the king chose to bind and lead the young men into the furnace were the top mighty men in the army at that time. These servants were burned up by the intense heat.

Some of you have had people who have tried to "throw you into the fire." Don't be bitter, be better. Rise above it and release them with the grace that only God can give you. He loves perfectly and forgives perfectly. We can't do that in our own strength, but with Jesus' love, we can. God is able to deal with our enemies. We don't have to fight that fight. Bless them as an act of obedience. This pleases God. (Don't wait for your feelings to catch up with you on this, they might not come.)

When we forgive others who have hurt us, it is like we step onto one of those conveyer belt walkways at the airport. We can just sail on by with grace and lightness, without the heavy burdens that unforgiveness and bitterness can bring. (These conveyers also get you to your destination more quickly, just as forgiveness does.) "For my yoke is easy and my burden is light" (Matthew 11:30).

Like I always say, *Take the HIGH ROAD, it has less traffic.*

I know forgiveness is easier said than done, and I am continually working on it. Forgiveness is something we will always be working on. As long as we are alive, we will have many opportunities to practice and improve upon forgiveness, because people are imperfect and hurt each other, knowingly or unknowingly.

The king was watching the three men in the fire, just as people are watching you go through your fire. Our testimony is being viewed, not only when we are on the mountain, but also in the valley.

"Then Nebuchadnezzar the king was astonished, and rose up in haste, and spake, and said to his counselors, 'Did not we cast three men, bound, into the midst of the fire?'" (I can just picture the king, puzzled and counting heads.) "They answered and said unto the king, 'True, O King.' He answered and said, 'Lo, I see *four* men *loose*, walking in the midst of the fire and they have no hurt; and the form of the fourth is like the Son of God'" (Daniel 3:24-25 KJV, emphasis added).

The fourth man is with you in your fire too. When you don't see Him, hear Him, or feel Him, He still remains present through the heat. As He was in Daniel's day, He is with you. He is called I AM, not I WAS.

I am grateful for that.

God is loosening your bondages in the fire. Things that can't go into this season with you are being removed. Things, situations, addictions, mindsets, and relationships that are not in your destiny are being loosed from you.

Don't worry, child. He is with you, even in the flames, to deliver you, strengthen you, refine you, and show you He is Emmanuel, God with us. He is near to you—today, tomorrow, and forever.

> "But as for me, the nearness of God is my good."
> (Psalm 73:28)

Then, King Nebuchadnezzar called them out of the fire by name.

The king called them out of the flames.

"Nebuchadnezzar then approached the opening of the blazing furnace and shouted, 'Shadrach, Meshach, and Abednego, servants of the Most High God, come out! Come here!'" (Daniel 3: 26).

Our enemies and others are paying attention to our fiery trials too, and how we come out of them. I have had people I didn't know very well approach me and tell me that they admired how I handled some tough things that I walked through. I didn't even realize they were watching. Our testimony is our life, a living epistle. The fact that you are still enduring through your trials is an encouragement, a torch in the night for others to see and continue on.

These young Hebrews did not come out of the fire running and screaming with their hair in flames. In fact, they stayed in the fire and had to be called out of it. When they came out, they were untouched by the fire's effects, except that their bindings were gone. No smoke, no burns, no damage. Nothing was lost except what had bound them. Everything was gained.

"So Shadrach, Meshach and Abednego came out of the fire, and the satraps, prefects, governors and royal advisors crowded around them. They saw that the fire had not harmed their bodies, nor was a hair of their heads singed; their robes were not scorched and there was no smell of fire on them" (Daniel 3:27).

The king even blessed their God! "Then Nebuchadnezzar said, 'Praise be to the God of Shadrach, Meshach, and Abednego, who has sent his angel, and rescued his servants. They trusted in him, and defied the king's command and were willing to give up their lives rather than serve or worship any god except their own God'" (Daniel 3:28).

Promotion comes after you come out from the fire. After the king called them out from the fire, he promoted the three courageous men and leaders of faith in the province of Babylon. He also made a decree that vindicated them and their faith in God.

You may have become exhausted from the intense heat of the fiery trial that you endured, or are enduring. But God is not slow in keeping His promises. He will promote you and bring you to that place, the sweet spot in life where your destiny intersects with your experiences, training, and entire being. You will breathe in fresh air and laugh again, too.

You will come out with a testimony of what the Lord has done. You will come out leaning on your Beloved. And, you will be promoted.

Recently, I was talking with my girlfriend who is going through cancer. She said that people always say that God won't give you more than you can handle. Then she said, "Of course He does! He always gives us more than we can handle, so we lean on Him and put our trust in Him, not in ourselves and our strength."

When I went through the fire of divorce, I felt the strength and nearness of my sweet Savior. I leaned on Him and drew from His love and strength. He seemed very quiet through all of it, but His quiet love settled the restless waters of my soul, just as He spoke to the waves of the storm and settled them.

> "The disciples went and woke him, saying, 'Lord, save us! We're going to drown!' He replied, 'You are of little faith, why are you so afraid?' Then he got up and rebuked the winds and the waves, and it was completely calm."
> (Matthew 8:25-26, NIV)

The love of Christ kept me sane. Every day and every hour, I needed His love, just as the Israelites needed manna for their daily nourishment in the desert. (See Exodus 16:14, NIV.) Manna doesn't look as desirable as dessert, or even fruit, I imagine. In the fiery season, the provision you have may not look like much, but it is from His hands and it will sustain you. The Israelites ate manna every day for forty years. My goodness, that is a very long time. I can't even eat the same kind of cereal every day for a month. It was bread from heaven, though, and it was good and sustaining.

Manna was very tiny, and had to be collected on a daily basis. It was not good to eat the next day. Daily bread. Daily strength. Daily healing. Jesus became our daily bread, sent from Heaven. We must partake of Him, spend time with Him each day, and be nourished by the fellowship of His Spirit.

During the divorce, I often fell into fear, doubt, and despair, with many tears. Christ gave me strength through His strength, which is rooted in perfect love.

> There is no fear in love. But perfect love drives out fear, because fear has to do with punishment. The one who fears is not made perfect in love.
> (1 John 4:18)

Then, I had to learn to adjust to being on my own. My friend and mentor, Joan Hunter, asked me how I was doing one day. I told her I felt like I was walking on water. She said, "You will be surprised at how hard that water under your feet becomes." I will never forget those powerful words. They gave me strength.

I had to put on my big girl pants and learn to do many things on my own that I had never done, nor thought I could do, such as being a provider, purchasing a home and a car, balancing finances (a work in progress), cutting hedges in the yard, and wrapping pipes in the winter. I'm still alive. I'm still learning every day.

One night, I asked my son Jacob (who was thirteen at the time) to learn alongside me how to wrap the outside plumbing pipes so they wouldn't burst in the Texas winter freeze. He was reluctant, at first, but then he became more helpful when he noticed what a feeble job I was doing. I also think it empowered him to know he was helping his mom and the family out. We were freezing out there, but hard at work with the foam and duct tape supplies. I told him, "Jacob, this is good training. You will need to know how to do this someday to take care of your wife and family." He stopped his work and said, "Mom, you just made this really awkward." I kept my mouth closed after that.

Also note God's provision and protection in the fire. Throughout our lives, we can look back and (hopefully) recognize the hand of God during some circumstances that could have derailed, or even destroyed us. I will share a few of mine with you.

I often look back to my childhood and remember the trials that my parents endured, including bankruptcy and uncertainty. One Saturday morning, I walked outside to get the morning newspaper for my parents, and I noticed that both our cars were missing out of the driveway. I ran inside and said, "Daddy, you won't believe this, but someone stole both of our cars!" He started laughing. He said, "Honey, they weren't stolen, they were repossessed because I couldn't pay for them anymore." He had been through so much and had three busy teenagers to provide for. I saw my dad courageously dust himself off and start over from scratch to provide for our family. Our neighbors brought us groceries for a while, which was amazing, until we got on our feet. Dad was raised in a loving family of twelve on a farm in North Dakota, and has always had the grit and determination to keep moving in the grace of God, no matter what. No matter how steep the climb, he faced the challenge, one single step at a time. His endurance and love strengthens my heart more than he will ever understand.

I see God's hand in many other situations in my life that could have been disasters for me. I thank Him for His loving rescue and help, even when I was running from Him. One spring break trip, my friends and I went to Padre Island, and then had the crazy idea to cross the border and go dancing in Matamoros, Mexico. While we were there dancing, we heard gun shots fired, and we all scattered out of the club. I got separated from my friends. They thought I was with someone else. I was in Matamoros without a ride back to Texas, and this was before cell phones! But I got a ride back with someone, a complete stranger, who was also staying in Padre.

I am grateful for His protection. When I was in my thirties, I was in seven car accidents within a two- or three-year span. (I was the passenger in each of them, in case you are thinking I must be a bad driver.) One day, my business partner and I had a meeting in Houston to go to. I had a really bad feeling all day and told her we needed to pray. I felt it so strongly and had trouble focusing on our meeting. On our way home from the meeting, we were hit from behind by a truck whose brakes had gone out. It was a huge, six-car pileup, and we were in the middle of it. The vehicle was totaled. The freeway was shut down, and we were put on stretchers and taken to the hospital in an ambulance. I was terrified, thinking of my little ones at home with the babysitter the whole time.

When we got to the ER, the paramedics took my friend's stretcher in first and told me they would be right back. The ER was overcrowded and they didn't have a spot for my stretcher. I wasn't thrilled about being left alone in a running ambulance. I was strapped down to the spinal backboard in a neck brace, unable to move anything but my eyes, I began to have a panic attack. It may sound silly, but I began to sing aloud the childhood song, "Jesus Loves Me" to calm myself. It worked, and His peace settled in the ambulance like a warm blanket. (Try it sometime. There is something so comforting about that song and the simplicity of the love of our Savior.)

My friend and I had to have therapy for our necks and backs, but we were alive and saved by the hand of God. That same day, at the exact time of our accident, a dear friend and founder of the church I attended, Reverend Henry Alloway, called my mom and asked, "Is Angela okay?" He said that for some reason, God told him to pray for my protection all day long, and he said the burden had just lifted. Neither one of them knew at that time about our wreck, but it was at the exact time that the accident was over. God had raised up this mighty prayer warrior to stand in the gap for the saving of my life!

Intercession

With a flaming sword,
I'll pierce the night
Wielding His weapons
With all my might
For those whose lives have been undone
To secure justice and victory
That's already been won!

—Angela Pollock

Chapter 2
Have your Senses Trained in the Fire

The last season was a difficult time to navigate, both for myself and for many people whom I know. It was difficult to see the path I was walking and get my bearings. I kept asking, "Where am I, Lord? Where am I going?" I went through a divorce after twenty-two years of marriage and with five children. There are no easy divorces, and it is hard on everyone involved. I felt dizzy, like I had been blindfolded and spun around and around about one hundred times, like in a Pin-the-tail-on-the-donkey game, then expected to walk straight and hit the target.

What happens when one of your senses is hindered or damaged? Your other senses kick into overdrive and become fine-tuned and more highly trained. They increase their normal capacity. The deaf learn to look more carefully for cues with their vision to determine what is going on around them. They watch peoples' facial expressions and body language very closely, and pay attention to lights and other external cues. They also use their sense of touch a great deal to feel the vibrations around them. The deaf are very good at reading lips. (I don't usually watch someone's lips, unless I am admiring their color of lip gloss.)

The blind have an incredible sense of hearing that has been heightened out of necessity. My friend, Missy, has a precious little two-year old daughter who is completely blind. Little Livvy has truly trained her other senses to discern her environment. She is amazing and gifted. She has an incredible sense of hearing and picks up music very quickly. She sings brand new songs with perfect pitch. Little Livvy also stomps her feet when she walks to help her judge where her boundaries are, and navigates that way impeccably. She will often reach out to hug you even though she cannot see a thing. She moves boldly, without trepidation, because she trusts her fine-tuned senses. She is a fearless little bundle of joy in this world. I can't wait to watch her bloom.

My most recent season–the season of fire–was a time to gain discernment and train my senses. God will always get the full mileage out of your fiery season. You may not realize until years later when you discover the gold that was produced in you in the heat.

Hebrews 5:14 (KJV) states, "But strong meat belongeth to them that are of full age, even those who by reason *of use* have their senses exercised to discern both good and evil" (emphasis added).

Of use in this verse means:
1. Habit, whether of body or mind
2. Power acquired by custom, practice, use

Power comes from practice. Practice comes in the trials. We desperately need to have our senses trained for the days we are living in. Soldiers are extensively trained in the area of specialty they will be serving in. Athletes also live a life of sacrifice and intense training. Twenty minutes a day on a treadmill is not going to cut it if you are headed for the Olympics. A commander in the military would not send a soldier into battle who just walked off the street in blue jeans to enlist. There is a cost that comes with the calling.

God will allow certain strenuous life experiences to come into our lives. We all need unique training that is suited and specific to our individual callings. God wants us to be equipped and prepared. Your testimony will help many people who can relate to what happened to you and be encouraged by how you came out of it.

I have found that each trial seems to get more steep, like the incline adjustment on a treadmill. This is part of the training. Muscles don't grow unless they are pushed and maxed out. When you are working out with weights, you don't see much difference on a day-to-day basis. Then, one sweet day, you catch a glimpse of your fine self in the mirror and are shocked at the growth. It takes time. It takes work. The trials that God has allowed me to walk through in the last few years would have crushed me twenty years ago. We don't go from flat to a steep incline on a treadmill overnight (at least I don't). Our incline is increased in subtle increments as our walk deepens with the Lord. Every year seems a bit steeper, in my experience, but every year, I hope to be stronger (and wiser) than the year before.

He is working endurance into us during these steep climbs and trials. So much is accomplished in us through the fiery trials as we keep our eyes on God and allow His work to work in us. So much glory and goodness is truly waiting on the other side of your fire.

When I look back on the trials (usually not during them), I thank God for the hard times. I thank Him for the rocky climbs that He brought me through. I thank Him that He didn't give me soft, pink bunny slippers to walk in. My feet have become bloody at times, and toughened at times. (Pedicures tend to help this.) It hasn't always been rosy, but I am stronger because of it. I want to use every pain I have felt in life for His gain.

> You are stronger than you think.

We need to refrain from comparing our training to that of those around us. We need to refrain from whining, grumbling, and complaining when the road gets steep. Can you imagine an Olympic athlete complaining to his coach about how hard he is being trained in comparison to his friends who are sitting home on the couch, texting all day long? That would be ridiculous. We are in a race that is not seen by this world. The training can be tough for the calling, but our Father is such a good dad. He wants us prepared physically, mentally, emotionally, spiritually, and financially.

The destiny He has for you is very special. It's like when people bring out their finest china for Thanksgiving dinner. You are set apart, reserved, for a special purpose. You will display the glory of God in your life and through the gifts He has given you.

Yield to the Fire.
Yield to the Training.
Your Senses are being Sharpened.

Sometimes, my kids ask me how to hear God's voice. I say it takes training and practice. I'm still learning. I believe He speaks to His kids, all of them. He created us to have fellowship with Him and to have a beautiful relationship with Him. Some people believe it is intuition, but I refer to it as the Holy Spirit.

We are spirits, with a soul and live in a body. In this day and age, the physical body is so glorified that sometimes we minimize the spiritual aspect of who we really are and will be for all eternity. Of course, it is important to nurture and strengthen our physical temple. It is a machine, a vehicle that needs to be healthy and fit. I see people spending hours a day at the gym, which is awesome, but what if we spent the same amount of time developing what is going on in the inside, in our spirits?

> The flesh is temporal.
> The spirit is eternal.
> The spirit has no wrinkles.
> Thank you, Lord.

There are times when your spirit overrides your mind and takes over. I remember the day my daughter Sarah and I were on our way to the airport to catch a flight to Los Angeles. We were really excited to go. I always say a quick pray over the plane and flight before we travel, but this time it came out a little different. As I was driving, I prayed aloud, "Lord, if there is anyone getting on our flight today that should not be on our plane, I ask you to please remove him! Amen." Sarah looked at me immediately and asked, "Why did you pray that, Mom?" I said "I don't really know. I have never done that before."

Well, we were all buckled in on the plane and ready for take-off, when a man stood up and started yelling and cussing at the top of his lungs. He was one row in front of us. Sarah's pretty blue eyes got really big! We were praying to be sure. The flight attendants tried to calm him down and figure out what the commotion was about. He was mad about his relatives being separated on the plane. People offered to change seats with them, but he refused to settle down. There was a U.S. Marshal onboard too, and after this man's behavior escalated, three attendants ushered him off of our plane. Everyone clapped! And I knew that God had answered my unusual prayer.

One way to learn to hear God's voice is by experiencing failure. If you have ever sensed or heard an internal voice telling you to do, or not to do something, and you ignored it, and suffered from that denial, you know what I mean. I have learned a lot by my many failures.

I have decided I would rather err on the side of obedience than rationalizing away the tug on my heart. If I feel a nudge to do something, or say something to a particular individual, you better bet your bottom dollar I'm going to be bold and say it. I have missed the boat too many times.

One day on a flight from Houston, there was a very famous actor on my flight. People were getting pictures with him and getting his autograph, but I just watched. He was in first class, and I just said hello when I passed him on my way to the economy section. Well, during the whole flight, I felt a strong burden for him. I felt that he needed prayer for his health, although he was a very physically strong man and seemed to be in perfect health. I struggled with what to do with this feeling, and eventually I wrote a note to him, explaining what I felt the Holy Spirit was impressing on me about him and his situation. I thought I might be bold enough to give it to him at the baggage claim. But I never saw him at the baggage claim. The burden remained so strong. I felt he needed prayer, and I did pray for him. Tragically, about two weeks later, this famous actor died. Everyone was in shock because he was the epitome of health and strength. I believe it was a heart attack.

Maybe my note wouldn't have changed a thing, but maybe it would have. Maybe it would have caused him to make a doctor's appointment that he had been putting off. Maybe it would have brought comfort to him to know that the Creator of the Universe saw him and cared enough to tell a complete to stranger to pray for him. As for me, I felt regret that I had missed the opportunity.

I decided to persevere more boldly in the future in prayer and with timely messages for others.

Another lesson on listening occurred when I was younger. I was going for a run one steamy Texas summer day. I had on shorts and was headed for the door, when I felt a nudge, a whisper, to go change into my lime-green, flannel-lined parachute warm-up pants that were popular in the 80s. Needless to say, I argued with God on this one. God doesn't really argue back. He gently gives us pearls of wisdom, and it is up to us to receive or reject them.

I didn't want to sweat in the Texan sauna-like weather. However, despite my arguing, I did go change. I listened.

I went on my run, and I know people could hear me coming a mile away with the swooshing sound of those parachute pants. They were ridiculous. Well, a little yappy dog heard me too, chased me down, and bit my leg. The good news is, even though I felt the bite, the dog's teeth could not penetrate the layers of nylon parachute and flannel that I was sporting. I had to giggle at the goodness of God that afternoon. I was also thankful the dog wasn't a Rottweiler.

God can speak through dreams too. We must pay attention to the instruction He seals up at night to His children. Six months before the horrible September 11 tragedies, I had a dream that planes were hijacked and turned mid-air into buildings to destroy them. It was very vivid and scary. I shared it with our prayer team and we prayed. At the time, it seemed as if the United States was too safe for such a hijacking to occur. Then, that awful morning came, and I watched the news in horror. I know of others who had similar dreams prior to that day.

Not too long after 9/11, two of my daughters and I were in New York City. My girls had been waiting all day to visit just one store on 5th Avenue. They took their usual number of hours doing their makeup and changing outfits, and we were all set to walk out of our hotel. Suddenly, I felt a caution in my spirit. It was as if a father had held out his hand in front of his kids before crossing a street and said, "Hold on a second, wait for the light to turn green."

Well, the caution I felt that day was very strong. I wondered if I was just being fearful because of the recent 9/11 tragedies. We waited, and prayed. I called for reinforcement prayer as well. Then, after about twenty minutes, I felt the caution lift, and said, "Let's go." My girls asked, "Are you sure, Mom?" I assured them that I felt complete peace.

So, we grabbed a taxi and went to shop at the only store on 5th Avenue they wanted to go to. After about thirty minutes of shopping, we walked out front to find the street full of firetrucks and ambulances, and the sidewalks packed with people. I asked around to find out what was going on. Finally, someone told me there had been a gas leak, but it had been fixed. Thank you, God. He knew the one store we were going to. He was looking out for not only us, but all of the people in that busy area.

I believe His angels were dispatched as we all prayed. You may see the results of your caution signs and prayers, as we did that day in NYC, or maybe not. You may never know the reason, but it is still worth it to obey. Blessings follow obedience. Believe that He is for you, with you, speaking to you, warning you, cheering you on, loving you, and guiding you on to succeed in all that you put your hands to do.

Faith is a substance. Grab hold of it and run!

> "Now faith is the substance of things hoped for,
> the evidence of things not seen."
> (Hebrews 11:1 KJV)

One more story of God's intervention occurred when my son Jacob was born. During labor, my epidural went drastically wrong, and they had to discontinue it. I was begging for drugs and they gave me something in my IV. Shortly after that, baby Jacob arrived. That night, the nurses kept checking on me because my blood pressure had crashed. I recovered and rested. In the middle of the night, the nurse brought Jacob in to me to nurse, and she turned on all the lights in the room. At the time, I thought that was too much, but I am so glad all the lights were on. When I held my little bit, he stopped breathing and turned blue! If that nurse would not have turned on all the lights, I would have assumed that he was sleeping, as newborns do! The doctors were called in for the Code Blue alert and they had to keep him there overnight, his very first night in the real world. I was so scared, but still groggy from labor and drugs. My husband was wiped too. I knew I needed to call for prayer reinforcements, because I was not at the top of my game in this condition. This was B.C. days (before cell phones) and it was long distance to call from the hospital to where my family lived. So, I called upon the Great Physician. I asked God to wake someone up to pray for Jacob so that he wouldn't die, but live. I trusted Him to take care of this tough situation.

He did live, and the next morning we got to love on our little miracle. When we got home, I received a phone call from my pastor's wife, Pastor Ginny. She asked, "How is Jacob"? I told her he was perfect. She said, "Well, God woke me up last night and said, 'Pray for Jacob that he won't die, but live.'" I said, "You're the one?" I told her the story, and it was about the same time that I cried out to God that she had prayed. I knew God would take care of it, but I never expected to know who it was that received that call from Heaven. I thought it might be someone on the other side of the world.

I am forever thankful that Ginny's senses had been trained through the years to hear God, and to listen to that still, small voice. Sometimes, it so still and so small that you think it is just one of your own thoughts.

Training and refining will occur in the fiery trials we endure. The fire is uncomfortable, but there is much value in the fire.

Chosen Flower

velvet petals
intoxicating aroma
fearfully made
unfurled beauty
promise and hope
deepest of love
nature's treasure
...a rose

—Angela Pollock

Chapter 3
Worship in the Fire

One of my mottos is: "Worship when it's hot, so you can bloom when it's not."

What we do in the fire affects us when we come out of it. Unfortunately, most of our trials are not as quick as the service at the beloved In-N-Out Burger restaurants. Hang in there, friend, you will come out.

The seeds of grumbling or complaining, or of praise and abiding, will bear fruit on the other side of the trial. We can determine to come out stronger.

Our worship does many things. In the fire, though, I believe it does even more. It gets more "bang for the buck." *It also gets the attention of God and Heaven.* We are surrounded by a great cloud of witnesses. (See Hebrews 12:1-2.) Our worship confuses the enemy on a sunny, carefree day, but just think what it does to him when we are worshiping our Lord through the most painful seasons. The fire sanctifies us, burns off the dross, and draws us closer to Him.

Worship is our compass in the fire. The heat can be very disorienting, and the one true way to regain focus is by worshiping the King of Kings. The perspective of His greatness and omnipotence, in relation to our temporary, yet painful, situation quickly changes the scenery of our heart. He must increase and we must decrease.

> "For thus saith the Lord God, the Holy One of Israel; In returning and rest shall ye be saved; in quietness and confidence shall be your strength: and ye would not."
> (Isaiah 30:15 KJV)

It is confidence in Him that gives us strength.

Have you ever seen a flower that is blooming through a crack in an old sidewalk? I marvel at that and want to ask that flower, "How did you get here, little sweetie? How did you manage to push through all that rock and dryness and exert your strength to bloom, just to brighten someone's day?" I see many people like that too, who have endured unspeakable circumstances. I'm amazed that their heart is still beating and that they are still breathing. And some are even smiling. They chose to bloom, even in very ugly, dark places. I want to ask them how they allowed love to unfold the petals of their life.

They blessed their Creator and dumbfounded their enemies.

God's grace is sufficient.

Likewise, there are beautiful, wild roses that bloom in the desert. It is a beautiful and amazing phenomenon. In the driest of places in life, where there seems to be no water, no answer, no breakthrough, we can still bloom. He will cause our roots to go as deep as is necessary to search for Him and His peace. Those who seek Him will find Him. You will be satisfied.

> "I love those who love me,
> and those who seek me find me."
> (Proverbs 8:17, NIV)

The fragrance of a rose is amazing. It is my favorite flower. Some flowers are beautiful to look at, but they have no fragrance. I want my heart to be filled with a fragrance for Sweet Jesus, and for life and others.

When we worship through our fire, it pleases the Lord. I know this with all of my heart. I have felt this deep in my being. I can't say I have always done it, but when I have, it changes things. Worshipping God may not change your circumstances immediately, but it will change you. It will deepen your relationship with the Father.

It honors Him.

I believe our expressions of love reach Him as a fragrance. His love is so unconditional, and I want to be more like Him. I want to love Him and worship Him just as deeply in the sunshine as in the storms.

I want my life to be the alabaster box that is poured out unto Him who alone is worthy.

I love the story in Matthew about the woman with the alabaster box.

"While Jesus was in Bethany, in the home of Simon the Leper, a woman came to Him with an alabaster jar of very expensive perfume, which she poured on his head as he was reclining at the table. When the disciples saw this, they were indignant. 'Why this waste?'" (Matthew 26:6-10, NIV).

The woman who did this for Jesus was looked down upon as foolish for wasting such costly perfume, but Jesus honored her very highly for it. The disciples were furious. They thought it should have been sold to help the poor. It seemed foolish, unnecessary, wasteful, and probably strange. In this account, Jesus was trying to relax and eat with His close group, yet this woman approached uninvited and did something bold, unusual, and extraordinary.

He told everyone that she was preparing Him for burial and that she would be honored throughout the world. There were some negative vibes going on in the room because of this woman's extravagant and costly worship. "Aware of this, Jesus said to them, 'Why are you bothering this woman? She has done a beautiful thing to me. The poor you will always have with me, but you will not always have me'" (Matthew 26:10-11, NIV).

Not everyone will "get" your worship or your path, but you'll be in good company. I don't know what the woman with the perfume had gone through, but when she met Jesus' eyes of perfect love, there was no cost too great to be given for the Master. Her worship and perfume touched much more than His head. It touched His heart. The very heart of God.

Isn't it amazing to think that we can affect His heart?

We can bless the Lord. Every day. He sups on our praise. What you have given to God is seen by Him as a "beautiful thing" as well. When you pour out your love and song to Him, He inhabits your being. (Even if you can't sing, like me.)

In the fire, worship is a sacrifice and goes against the grain of our flesh, but the more we do it, the more we are sanctified. Remember Job, and all of the horrific things he endured? Yet, he refused to curse God. The Lord returned to Job more than he could've ever dreamed of.

He will turn your bitter to better.

The prophet Isaiah wrote:

> The Spirit of the Sovereign Lord is on me, because the Lord has anointed me to proclaim good news to the poor. He has sent me to bind up the brokenhearted, to proclaim freedom for the captives and release from darkness for the prisoners, to proclaim the year of the Lord's favor and the day of vengeance of our God, to

comfort all who mourn, and provide for those who grieve in Zion—*to bestow on them a crown of beauty instead of ashes,* the oil of joy instead of mourning, and a garment of praise instead of a spirit of despair. They will be called oaks of righteousness, a planting of the Lord for the display of his splendor.

(Isaiah 61:1-3 NIV, italics added)

Beauty from ashes? I used to read that verse and ponder. How could God make something beautiful from ashes? My kids and I make s'mores often and so I have studied these ashes. They seem pretty useless and ugly when you look at them. They are messy too. The Lord of all creation has a way of turning the ashes of our broken, dark place, where life didn't seem fair and life didn't seem fun, and making us new again.

New means new. It doesn't even resemble the old. New life, new joy, new hope, and new dreams will come. He will breathe life into every cell of your DNA, child.

Yours

What can I bring You?
I'll bring you my song ...
The praise from my lips
  All the day long.

What can I give You?
The King, who has all?
A heart, undivided
  To answer Your call.

My feet, to Your service,
To go where You send.
To seek out the lonely,
Who just need a friend.

—Angela Pollock

Chapter 4
Stay Low in the Fire

In the natural sense, it can save your life if you stay "low" in a fire. We have all heard the advice, "Stop, drop, and roll." Smoke rises, so if you stay low, you can crawl out and survive.

In the fiery trials of life, it helps to stay low as well. During the last two years, I had one blow after another that knocked me down for a little bit. I would get hit with something, lose my balance, go down, then get back up slowly. It seemed that as soon as I stood up and recovered from one big hurt and brushed myself off, I got hit again. The process repeated. Stand up, regain some strength, then boom, another hit.

At times, I felt so low that it seemed like I was crawling out of the fire with carpet under my fingernails. But I was determined to come out of the fire, even if I had to come out crawling.

> If you can't run, walk.
> If you can't walk, crawl.
> Just keep moving.
> Don't stay put in the heat.

I loved being a stay-at-home mom and raising my babies more than anything in the world, even though it was challenging. We had five little ones, close in age and heights like stair steps. Every day was an adventure. I remember one morning, I walked into the kitchen to make coffee and found my toddlers painting all of the kitchen cabinets with paint brushes and sour cream! They had seen me paint and remodel our house so much and wanted to contribute.

Another day, I was at the checkout line in the grocery store and my kids were all bouncing around like kids do with all that candy in view. The lady behind us was looking on, huffing and sighing with impatience. Finally, she said, "If I were you, I would be pulling my hair out." I just looked back at her, smiled, and said, "Well, good thing God gave me a lot of hair." He gave me a lot of grace too.

These are funny stories, but when our children were little, I also went through a really difficult season. I don't really know how long it lasted, to be honest. Life was blurry for me then. The colors of my world became dull.

I didn't actually know I was depressed until I went to the doctor for a sore throat. I saw a nice Indian doctor, whom I had never met, at the after-hours clinic. He looked at my throat, then he looked me in the eyes and said, "How are you?" (Those are very powerful words to ask someone. Ask, and *wait* for their response. Sadly, it rarely happens these days.) Well, his little question of "How are you?" opened up the floodgates for me. I began to weep. He asked me if I cried every week and I said yes. He asked me if I cried every day and I said yes. He said, "That's not normal." I said, "It's not?"

Depression is like sinking sand, a slow, squeezing descent, and you lose sight of what normal is until someone speaks up and intervenes as a virtual plumb line.

My family also went through brutal financial hardships. My husband at the time had a job, but we were struggling. I was in extreme anxiety, fight-or-flight-mode *most of the time.*

When checking out at the grocery store, I would pray and pray for the credit card machine to say "Accepted" when paying, but very often it was declined. I always had a flashback of the scene from *Terms of Endearment* where the mom (Debra Winger) is scrambling, with her kids in tow, to pay for her groceries. The grocery clerk comes on the intercom and says, "The lady doesn't have enough money."

At the checkout, I had all of the groceries bagged up to go, but then the terminal flashed that dreaded word: DECLINED. It put a ding in my pride, for starters, but I had to leave the store, *and* all the groceries, with my sweet little five-year-old daughter, Adrien, holding my hand as we walked to the car. (She had stared at all those goodies on the conveyer belt and wondered why they weren't coming home with us.)

I always tried my best to hold it together for the kids' sake and be positive, but that day I just broke. We got in the car and my tears began to release in utter frustration and weariness of the long season of financial stress. I couldn't contain my thoughts and said out loud, "What's the point?"

Sweet Adrien looked at me with her big blue eyes and light blond hair (she looked like Cindy Lou Who in the Dr. Seuss movie) and said some words I will never forget. She asked, "What's the point of what, Mommy?"

I continued in my negativity. "The point of everything," I said quietly.

She looked at my sad eyes and said, "How about doing it for Jesus?"

I asked, "Do what for Jesus?"

"Everything", she said.

God had to remind me, through my pure little five-year-old, about the perspective that could get me through any hardship I will ever encounter. In the good and in the bad, do it all for Him who is worthy.

Endure, for Him.
He endured for us.

Now, I watch for the times when someone in my line at the grocery store gets that dreaded "declined" message. Being able to pay for that person's groceries is a great joy, knowing how stressful that situation can be. One time, I saw a couple who had tried every credit card in the man's wallet. I offered to pay for their groceries, but the man refused. Then, he tried another card. It also declined. I offered again. He said no again and again, but his wife had a "yes" in her eyes, along with tears. They were stressed.

I shared with him that the situation was temporary. I also told him I had been on the other side of this coin so many times, and that I would love to help him because God had helped me through so much. Finally, he agreed and thanked me. As he shared his trial, we all cried, including the cashier. It was a glorious mess!

In spite of His faithfulness to me, I still struggled with trusting God through different, tough seasons. I began to have panic attacks and other various health problems with my heart. Once, on a flight back from NYC, I had severe chest pains and my left arm was numb. The pain was so severe that I was in tears. The flight attendant spoke with me, then got on the intercom and asked if there was a doctor on the plane. Well, there was one—two rows behind me! He sat in the aisle, pulled out his stethoscope, and monitored me the whole flight. I was fine. (In looking back, I recall that my carry-on suitcase, which was overloaded with high heels, may have been a contributing factor to this incident. I could barely lift it into the overhead compartment, and probably strained a muscle. Lesson learned: travel light, or lighter at least.)

Another time, I had severe chest pains, so I sent my kids to the neighbors to get help. Then, I called 9-1-1, but they never came. I called them back and asked them if they were lost, and they said no. Well, they never showed. My neighbors did come and tried their best to settle me down. Jehovah Rapha (God, My Healer) came too. He is always present, on time, and knows where you live!

I lost a lot of weight, and I was already pretty thin. I was extremely depressed. I saw people laughing and couldn't imagine what was funny in life. I had physical problems, but I believe now that most of that was due to stress and oppression.

The stress in your life will manifest in your body, if not relieved in healthy ways. Tears are one way that the stress and hurts in our lives find escape. Studies have shown that there are chemicals found in emotion-based tears (not tears from onions) that act as natural painkillers. Often, people feel much better after a good cry.

Photographer Rose-Lynn Fisher says that tears are "the evidence of our inner life overflowing its boundaries, spilling over into consciousness. Wordless and spontaneous, they release us to the possibility of realignment, reunion, catharsis: shedding tears, shedding old skin." I came across her cool photos of tears as I was writing these pages, and was amazed by her curious study and photographs. She began to wonder if her tears of grief and laughter would differ from tears from cutting an onion. She studied them under a microscope (magnified 10x and 40x) and photographed the images. Her work is called "Topography of Tears" and it is amazing to see the dramatic difference in the composition of tears of change, tears of grief, tears of laughter, etc. They look like artwork. (Fisher, Rose-Lynn. http://www.rose-lynnfisher.com/tears.html. Images and text copyright 2013-2015. Accessed 02/2016)

I was in the ER so many times that they knew my name, and they were not happy to see me. I was a freak. All of the problems I was having brought a fear of death within me. I was very afraid of dying and not being able to be a mom for my children. I was even afraid to go to sleep at night because the physical symptoms and fear were increasing. I prayed every night that I would wake up to see another day, literally. One time in the ER, I had a bad reaction to the medicine they gave me and I really went off the deep end. My sweet daddy was right beside me through the chaos (while my precious mom juggled our kids). The doctor told him not to leave me alone for a second. I told my dad to go get help because the pain was so bad, but he refused to leave my side. So, I started screaming, "I'm going to die. Somebody help me."

My heart was hooked up to monitors and one doctor went and got several more doctors because something was wrong with my heart. I was yelling, "Where are the paddles? I'm about to die. Please bring me back, I have five little kids." My eyes were combing the room for the paddles that I had seen on all those medical shows on TV (I watched too much ER and George Clooney), but they were nowhere to be found. I asked again, "Where are the paddles? Are you prepared?" The doctor looked at me and calmly said (in a Texas accent), "Ma'am, you're in a hospital. If you're going to die, this is the best possible place for you to be." Well, I didn't appreciate his tone; it was too calm. I didn't think he was taking me seriously. (I guess I wanted someone to match my level of hysteria.)

My husband (at the time) came on the scene too. He had seen me act like this in childbirth five times before, so he wasn't startled. He calmly told me to focus on something and get a hold of myself. I tried. I took the TV remote and began turning the TV on and off a thousand times like a crazy woman.

Finally, I called my pastor and his wife (Pastors Brian & Ginny Baker/Church of the Savior) for prayer, while screaming that I was in the ER and about to die. The God Squad—three dear friends who are powerful prayer warriors, the equivalent of Navy Seals—showed up in a matter of minutes. The nurses were relieved too and quickly escorted them to my tiny room. They filled that space with great faith. My friends stormed Heaven's gates and gave the devil a black eye for messing with one of God's children. The atmosphere of Heaven quickly replaced the atmosphere of fear.

The staff was amazed at the peace that shifted the situation as well. I was even able to take a much-needed nap. They sent me home with medication for anxiety, but I never took it. (I am not against medicine to help symptoms at all. I just knew it wasn't for me.)

I found a peace that could never fit in a bottle and a love that saturated my cells. Yes, Jesus is the answer, my friend, even if you're not asking the question yet.

The power of God supernaturally healed my body. (I received a revelation of the deep love of God through the story of Jonah, but that will be in another book.)

When I went to a cardiologist for a checkup later, the nurse did an ultrasound on my heart. I asked her if everything looked okay. She said, "You have the heart of a lion."

I smiled and said, "Yes, the Lion of Judah."

Gentle Love

Love that is a gentle wind saying,
"Forget the stress and come worship me"
Love that looks past the hurts, and forgives.
Love that makes me want to run to Heaven
and peek at the glory of God,
so I might endure this race on Earth.
Love that gives me courage to face my enemies
and see them flee.
Love that bled for you and me.
And ...
Love that was small enough to fit in a manger,
yet large enough to save the whole world!

—Angela Pollock

I wrote this in the hospital in 1998, the night after delivering my precious son, Riley David. As I held my first son, swaddled in a felt Christmas stocking just a few days before Christmas, my heart was consumed with the love of God through His Son, and the son He gave me. It was a special, magical night that I will not forget.

Chapter 5
Obey His Direction in the Fire

During the fire, bondages will be broken off by the heat. God can multi-task like none other. He may show you relationships that are weighing you down and need to go. You may have relationships that are really pleasing to your soul, but if not God-ordained, they will not bring you closer to your destiny. They will not intersect with the plans and adventures written in the Lamb's Book of Life for you. They are "destiny delayers," as I like to say.

In college, I thought I had met the man of my dreams, but he wasn't in God's dream for me. He was a really good guy. God said he wasn't in my book, but I pleaded with Him to rewrite a few pages. He didn't waver. I had to say good-bye, and it felt like my heart had been ripped out of my chest. I didn't think I would ever get over this fine gentleman. Years later, I attended a woman's conference, and one of the speakers called me out and said, "You recently had to say good-bye to someone who was close to your heart. God wants you to know He saw that and He is proud of you." I thought that was an interesting word, and I turned to my sister and said, "I wonder who He is talking about." I only had a couple of boyfriends in college, so it should've been obvious, but I really had to think for a few minutes before I remembered that gut-wrenching experience. I was in shock at how the Lord had healed my sad heart and healed the scars.

He delights in our obedience. He takes note of everything we do.

God is not into BAND-AIDS;
They just don't stick to the heart.
He heals completely.

My mom and I were driving home from Arkansas one late night and we stopped for gas. When we tried to get back on the highway, we ended up on a parallel road instead. We were tired and we were delirious. We could not find a way to get back on the main freeway, even though we could clearly see it and were running directly parallel to it. It was like the Griswold European Vacation movie where Chevy Chase drives around the Big Ben roundabout at Parliament in London. They circled around and around and could not get over.

Every decision we make is important, and we need to trust in His guidance. Stay focused with those with whom you are called to breathe in this life. God will guide you in the fire. He will whisper wisdom to you. If you heed it, you will come out lighter and freer than you ever imagined. He may remove relationships and add new ones to strengthen and propel you to new heights. Soar with those who are eagles, even if you have to coast on their wind currents for a bit.

There is much wisdom in following a great mentor, holding up their arms, being an armor bearer to one who walks in a grace, a gift, or an anointing similar to what you have inside of you. Once you catch how great the view is from their vantage point, you will not want to return to those turkeys or bottom dwellers you may have been hanging out with for far too long.

If you feel like God is not giving you specific direction, then just stay the course. Stay in peace. That is how trust is built. He is such a great Father and wants you on the right path, even more than you want it for yourself. When you need a mile marker, you will get it.

I am so thankful for the new navigation systems, because previously I was always getting lost. I still get lost, even with the GPS, but not as often. I would frequently stop at gas stations and ask for directions on a road trip. They often said, "Yes, you are on the right track, just keep going." Then, I would drive for a while and stop again to ask for confirmation.

One time, I got so lost and my GPS had no signal. I ended up on some very back farm roads outside of Fort Worth. I was so distraught, and there was nothing around me but farms as far as I could see. I saw a herd of cattle in a pasture and stopped my car. I walked to the fence and stared at the big, black Angus steers as if to say, "Hey, fellas, can you help a girl out? I'm lost." They stared back at me. Cattle have such a peaceful way about them. They don't worry or stress. I thought they would settle me down, or at least give me some kind of sign, or a flick of their tail as to which direction to go. Not.

Then, I stumbled upon a gas station with three men in it. One man did not speak English, one said he had never heard of Interstate 45, and the other man said he had a GPS in his truck and would help me if I got into his truck. I said *adios* and left them in the dust quickly. Somehow, I found a highway. I know my angels are very busy and deserve a raise!

Sometimes along the journey, we can feel disheartened, confused, panicked, or just plain weary, if we don't feel a specific direction from the Lord. Keep cruising on. He is faithful to lead as the Good Shepherd that He is. He will go after the one little lamb out of ninety-nine who is straying or has been hurt, or even taken a wrong turn.

Most of us aren't exposed to shepherding or farming in this day we live in, but if you read Psalm 23, you will find it very comforting and beautiful. I have studied shows on TV about shepherding to gain a better perspective of Jesus' strong and gentle role as our Shepherd. The shepherd will lay his body down in the gate of the fold where the sheep are kept to protect them from their predators. Jesus laid down His body on the cross for His sheep, His children, as a ransom for us. He stood in the gap.

> "The Lord is my Shepherd, I lack nothing.
> He makes me lie down in green pastures,
> He leads me beside quiet waters,
> He refreshes my soul.
> He guides me along the right paths for his name's sake.
> Even though I walk through the darkest valley,
> I will fear no evil, for you are with me;
> Your rod and your staff, they comfort me.
> You prepare a table before me in the presence of my enemies.
> You anoint my head with oil;
> my cup overflows.
> Surely your goodness and love will follow me all the days of my life, and I will dwell in the house of the Lord forever."
> (Psalm 23)

He cares for you, little lamb.
Trust that.
Follow His leading and follow Him out from the fire.
He is with you, even if you feel alone.

Three things have helped me to hold onto a confidence that this world cannot take away:
1. *God has your heart.* If you allow Him, He will heal, strengthen, love, and protect it!
2. *God has your hand.* He will lead you, walk beside you, and have fellowship with you.

3. *God has your plan.* He has the blueprints to your life that will satisfy your DNA. He is faithful.

> "For I know the plans I have for you, declares the Lord, plans to prosper you and not to harm you, plans to give you hope and a future."
> (Jeremiah 29:11, NIV)

Good Shepherd

Lean into Me.
Lean into Me.
And you will find the answers near.

Lean into Me.
Lean into Me.
In my presence, there's no fear.

I love you, little lamb.
I chose you, my sweet friend.
I made you to walk with Me
  Closely, hand in hand.

Come away with Me.
Let love rapture your soul,
  And peace descend
On all you hold dear.

—Angela Pollock

Chapter 6
Don't Waste the Fire

No one knows just how hot your fiery trial is, that is, except the fourth man in the fiery furnace, who is walking beside you, just as He did with the Hebrew boys. You can dance through your trials with the grace of your Beloved and you will come out without the smell of smoke. That's when you know He has made a masterpiece of your heart; when you come out from the fire with a fragrance, not a stench.

Some people continue to gripe and complain about injustices done to them many years ago. They make it sound like it happened yesterday. Their wounds are still raw. We have to let it all go if we want to go higher in life.

A hot air balloon can only go so high until it has to release some baggage. Then, it can soar higher and effortlessly in the sky. Holding onto the past will always weigh you down and steal the fragrance that God wants to release in and through you.

Also, when you come out from the fire, you will have a new vision, a new awareness of those around you who have suffered through similar trials as you have. It's like you have a new radar or gift to pick up on those things. Some people are very lonely, though they may be speaking to thousands. I can often sense when people are depressed, even if they are smiling. I try to reach out and talk or pray with them when I can. I have walked through the dark fire of depression, so I recognize what it looks like in others. I am thankful that God allowed me to go through that valley, so I can help others who are suffering. He didn't send it, but He was with me through every minute of it.

Jesus learned compassion through the things He suffered. The Son of God suffered on this earth. I can't imagine what His parents went through, either. While it was an amazing gift to be given the privilege of raising Jesus and see the miracles He did, they also had to watch Him suffer, be despised, betrayed, and rejected. He is our intercessor. His greatest act of intercession was dying on the cross for us.

He understands what a life in the flesh can entail. He had to endure the cross. We have to go through the fire.

Go through.
Glory awaits us on the other side.

Going through the fire also produces endurance. Unfortunately, endurance is not something we can purchase on aisle eight at the grocery store. Believe me, if it were possible, I would've bought the whole shelf, because I have needed it! God knew I needed it too, and that is why He allowed me to go through some tough stuff in order to gain it.

Endurance must be walked out. There are no short cuts. It is not easy. I feel we must quit seeking to look for things to get "easier," and, instead, seek God to make us stronger.

When the Israelites were slaves in Egypt, Pharaoh's heart was hardened against them, time and time again. He commanded the taskmasters in charge of God's people, saying, "Ye shall no more give the people straw to make brick, as heretofore: let them go and gather straw for themselves" (Exodus 5:7 KJV). The increase of the work and demands put upon God's chosen people only made them stronger. Their exodus finally came, and they left with much spoil. Endurance pays off.

> "And not only so, but we glory in tribulations also: knowing that tribulation worketh patience; And patience, experience; and experience, hope: And hope maketh not ashamed; because the love of God is shed abroad in our hearts by the Holy Ghost which is given unto us." (Romans 5:3-5 KJV)

In 2 Timothy 2:3 (KJV) Paul instructs: "Thou therefore endure hardness, as a good soldier of Jesus Christ." Your endurance will be like a three-stranded cord that pulls someone out of the quicksand. Depression, suicidal thoughts, and other ailments are like quicksand. Most of the time, people bound in depression will not ask for help. If you say, "Call me if you need something," they will not call. You have to show up in your blue jeans and say, "I am here, and I am coming in to love and help you, and pull you out of this death trap."

However, words aren't always necessary. Your very presence is a gift to someone who is hurting. Just show up. Sometimes we just need a sincere hug or hand to hold, and exhale for a bit. Praying for someone, though, is a great gift of love that brings Heaven on the scene to exchange the darkness of the soul for the light of His presence and love.

> True love gets messy,
> gets in the trenches,
> gets inconvenienced,
> and simply loves.

I remember one day when I was at home, in tears, and a dear friend showed up in blue jeans with a bouquet of flowers in her hands with a note that read: "Love, Jesus." I thanked her and she said, "Don't thank me, it was His idea." She will never know how much that meant to me. It reminded me that *I was still visible to God*, even in my sadness.

The rate of suicide today is astounding and saddening. We have to be the hands and feet and voice of love for people. We must cross over the hidden lines of "private space" to help people navigate out of death and into life.

After graduating from Texas A&M University, I worked briefly at the A&M employee counseling center as an office manager. One of our clients called in one day to say thank you and goodbye. She had taken an overdose of her medication and was within minutes of her death. I kept her on the phone, speaking calmly to her, finding out what she had taken, and where she was so I could call 911 to her rescue. I would have transferred a suicidal patient immediately to one of licensed counselors, but our phone system was very tricky, and I had lost many calls before trying to transfer. I was not about to risk dropping someone's last attempt for help! I was able to convince her that her counselor would love to talk with her and see her again. I frantically motioned for the counselor's attention, even though she was in session with another patient. The counselor got on the phone and spoke so kindly with her while I called 911. They arrived at her house while she was still talking to her counselor. Then, they were able to pump her stomach, and she lived! She was treading the deep waters of her life, almost surrendering the fight. Heaven stepped in, angels stepped in, and people helped to be the life-preserver to this wearied soul. She came out of her intense fire and found new joy in her life too. I'm so thankful.

Shortly after this incident, our center was under review due to university budget cuts. Below is a portion of the letter that my boss sent to the university. (I just found this letter in an old box, as I was writing this book.) He explained the scary situation we just had, and thanked us for our professionalism in assisting this dear patient. He also states:

> *I know our program, like others, has been under close scrutiny during budget years. Because we are not a program with lots of "bells and whistles" or high daily visibility, it is sometimes difficult to appreciate the outcome of our services. I really believe that had our program not existed, this individual would be dead. I don't know what monetary value to place on a single human life, but if someone else can, please mark this one in the asset column.* —Dr. P.

God will have us in the right place at the right time, for the right season, and for the right reason. He is good!

Your test is wasted if you don't turn it into a testimony. Use it or lose it. All of your pain, all of your tears, your battles with sickness or mental struggles or divorce or financial problems—they can be turned into a weapon and used to slay giants for others who are suffering. All you have to show for it may not look like much, like a little rock. Rocks don't look too special, or too impressive, but young David, before he became king of Israel, had a handful of rocks, and that worked quite well for him! He slew the giant Goliath with what was in his hand and with the confidence he had gained from his previous battles of conquering lions and bears. (See 1 Samuel 17:34.) Remember your victories and use them! They will give you the confidence you need when you have a big, ugly giant staring at you in the face and taunting you.

Refuse to allow shame or pride to keep you from sharing what God brought you through. If you were abused, don't shrink back in the shame of that, because you can be the light to someone who is suffering. Think about how many thousands of people that

Joyce Meyer has helped by sharing her traumatic testimony of being abused by her father. If she would have kept her testimony in the closet of shame or anger, so many people would still be bound today.

> Use your fire for the greater good
> and the greater love.

The King of Kings is calling you out from the fire, just as King Nebuchadnezzar called Shadrach, Meshach, and Abednego. Just like them, you will come out without the smell of smoke upon you.

> You will come out better, not bitter.
> You'll come out wiser and stronger.

God is preparing You for the arena He has already prepared for you.

Strength looks good on YOU!

NEW

Fresh Start

New beginnings

Valley deep and wide

Recovery of all that's lost

Look up, light draweth nigh.

—Angela Pollock

Closing Words

I know I'm a rambling gal, but I am a Texan, after all, and we are born to talk. In closing, I want to encourage you if you are going through the fire, or have recently come out of one. You may be exhausted, dizzy, downcast, bewildered, and utterly spent, but if you are still breathing, you made it! Your destiny awaits you and is calling out to the only one who can fulfill it. And that is you.

You are not alone.
You are chosen and a beautiful child of God.
You may have been told that you were an "accident" or a "surprise" when you were born. Well, sweetie, you weren't an accident, and you weren't a surprise to God at all. He knew you before you were in your mama's belly and He wrote out your destiny, which no one can erase.

I pray that your soul be healed of all words (said in ignorance or malice) that wounded your soul, or caused a spirit of rejection to come in. I declare healing and wholeness over your body, mind, and spirit.

You are not rejected, but cherished by your loving Creator.

Many times I've said, "Lord I believe your Word that says joy comes in the morning, but is it morning yet, God?"

Yes, healing is a process, like many things in life. And sometimes the process is short...so hang in there!

I want to pray now for you and all those who are in a fiery situation. Lord, I thank you for all the precious people reading this prayer.

I pray that the perfect love of Jesus would be poured out upon you at this very moment. I speak the peace and healing power of God to fill you up. I declare hope to the hopeless. I pray for healing of all trauma that your soul has ever suffered. I declare wholeness and newness of life. I am believing for victory for you. I declare blessings will chase you down and overtake you.

I pray for healing of your mind and memories. I bind up tormenting thoughts and memories that would keep you awake at night. I declare sweet sleep over you and peace in your home. I speak strength to you—body, soul, and spirit.

I speak the precious blood of Jesus over your past, your present, and your future. I pray that you would receive the grace of God to forgive those who have hurt you, even as a child, and also the grace to forgive yourself.

I speak trust and security to be returned to fortify your heart. I pray healing and restoration over your broken heart. I speak the manifestation of the presence of God in your life.

You are Cherished
Chosen
and Significant!
Amen

A Personal Invitation

Precious one,

Today is the day of salvation, now is the hour of power.
Say yes.

If you do not have a true relationship with Jesus, the Son of God, I urge you to call upon Him today. His love has been chasing some of you all your life and you keep running. Let Him catch you. Turn around and fall into His open arms. Nothing you have ever done can separate you from His love. Nothing in this world will ever satisfy like His love.

You can speak to Him as you do a friend, from your heart. Ask Him to forgive you of your sin, enter your heart, and become the Lord of your life. He died for your sins. No human has the power to cleanse us of our sin, guilt, shame, and regret. Only Jesus can. No human can love you with a perfect love. Only Jesus can.

Don't over-think God. He's not that complicated. Some very intelligent people miss out on a relationship with God because they are so smart. They think it is foolish to believe Him in simplicity as a child. A little child can come to Him. He desires you. He sings over you. He rejoices over you.

I sat on a Southwest Airlines flight one day, next to a very intelligent businessman. It was a red-eye flight, and I hadn't had any coffee yet, so I wasn't feeling my chatty self. But I did find out through casual conversation that he was a chemist. His company transformed certain elements in the earth into gold! I was quite intrigued, but I reclined my seat as soon as the wheels were up and decided to rest my eyes. Well, God had another agenda!

He whispered to my heart to talk to this businessman next to me. He said, "Tell him about me." Well, as much as the Creator of this Universe has done for me, I said, "Yes sir," without hesitation.

I put my seat back into the upright position, looked at this man boldly, straight in the face, (in my pre-coffee state) and asked, "Do you believe in Jesus"? (I am not normally so direct.)

He looked at me, looked out the window, then said, "No, no, I don't."

I think I said "Hmm," or something profound like that, then reclined my seat backward again and closed my eyes. I had a quick conversation with God. "Lord," I said, "I'm not trying to hurt your feelings, but so far this is not going too good. He does not believe in you ... at all!" (Take note: God can handle rejection. He has been dealing with this for quite a while.)

I felt that God was saying, "Exactly, that's exactly why I want you to share with him about me!" I asked God to give me wisdom, because this man was much smarter than I was and I needed God's help to relay what I was feeling.

I told the man that he had a lot in common with Jesus. That caught his attention. I said, "You know, Jesus was a chemist too." The man said, "I thought he was a carpenter." (So, he had heard of Jesus, somewhat.) "Yes," I said, "He was a carpenter, but also a chemist. He turned water to wine." I gave him a couple of other examples that he could relate to, and I think he was intrigued at the scientific properties of the miracles that Jesus did. Jesus did some pretty cool, out-of-the-box stuff, and still does! I have seen countless, undeniable miracles. I shared with this gentleman some stories of the naturally supernatural God I know, gave him some more resources to check out, and told him to give Jesus a chance. I pray that he does.

If you open the door of your heart just a crack, His love will flood in. A faith the size of a grain of mustard seed is all that He requires to get the beautiful journey started.

If you are afraid of erring, then "err" on the side of faith. Trust that there is a Holy God who knows your name, loves you, and created you to do amazing and beautiful things that will bless your soul, others, and Him. Believe He is crazy about you and loves you with a fiery love. He is on your side and wants you to live in wholeness and victory.

Life is short, but eternity is forever.
I pray that you allow Him to love you.
You won't ever regret it.

With Much Love,
Angela

About the Author

Angela M. Pollock delights in sharing a message of hope, creativity and humor with audiences of all ages. Angela believes that the love, power, and miracles of God should be a supernaturally natural part of our everyday lives. She desires to see people become unlocked and freed to run in the destiny that they were created to fulfill and enjoy. She is a single mother of five, an entrepreneur, and speaker. She enjoys travel and nature, and is addicted to chocolate and sunsets!

For more information:
Please visit www.angelapollock.com

To book Angela Pollock for:
—speaking engagements
—ministry events
—and prayer requests,

Email:
contactangelapollock@gmail.com

Endorsements

Vibrantly alive and aware in the Holy Spirit is how I describe Angela. We have had the joy of seeing her grow in the Spirit since she was a teen, and have rejoiced in our hearts every time we see her, a mature woman, still on fire in her heart and life for Jesus!

Pastors Ginny and Brian Baker
Church of the Savior, Texas

I'm so excited that Angela has written a book about going through the fires of life. The timing could not be more perfect as we have a world that is going through so much turmoil and, consequently, is causing the American family and culture to go through undue stress, extreme pressure, and trial as by fire! Reading through these pages of Angela's book, From the Fire, will help you to emerge from your fire without even a smell of smoke!

Pastor Eileen Hackleman
www.familyfaithchurch.com
Family Faith Church, Pastors Jeff & Eileen Hackleman, Texas

I have known Angela Pollock for many years and I love her! She is a beautiful woman, loving mom, kind friend, and dedicated Christian. Her book From the Fire is her own life story. She shares how she went through the "valley of the shadow of death" and came out the other side a stronger, better person. Few people are fortunate enough to go through life without enduring times of intense suffering, rejection, or difficulty. However, all Christians have a loving God who watches over them and the Holy Spirit living inside them who can and will deliver them from every evil and perfect His love in them if they will trust and obey Him. As believers go through the fire, they become one with the fire and with Him who is light. Read and meditate on this book and you will gain new insight and discover new ways to respond to your fiery trials and come through a totally new person!

>   Joan Hunter
>   Author/Evangelist
>   *www.joanhunter.org*
>   *Founder and President of Joan Hunter Ministries*

Angela Pollock is one of the most literal lovers of God that I know. She's a constant flame for Christ, yielding to the Spirit in everything and obedient, regardless of the feat. Angela is armed with a powerful gift of intercession and a proven, accurate gift of prophecy. The many trials of her life have made her a permanent fire for the Kingdom of God, and underneath her beauty are hot coals of passion to see the captives set free!

>   Pastor Jennifer Walker
>   *www.womenofwarministry.com*
>   *The Prayer Room Church, Pastors Robert & Jennifer Walker*
>   *The Woodlands, Texas*

www.ingramcontent.com/pod-product-compliance
Lightning Source LLC
LaVergne TN
LVHW051158080426
835508LV00021B/2690